A DAY IN THE LIFE OF A TEACHER

THIS EDITION

Produced for DK by WonderLab Group LLC
Jennifer Emmett, Erica Green, Kate Hale, *Founders*

Editor Maya Myers; **Photography Editor** Nicole DiMella; **Managing Editor** Rachel Houghton;
Designers Project Design Company; **Researcher** Michelle Harris; **Copy Editor** Lori Merritt;
Indexer Connie Binder; **Proofreader** Susan K. Hom; **Series Reading Specialist** Dr. Jennifer Albro

First American Edition, 2025
Published in the United States by DK Publishing, a division of Penguin Random House LLC
1745 Broadway, 20th Floor, New York, NY 10019

Copyright © 2025 Dorling Kindersley Limited
24 25 26 27 10 9 8 7 6 5 4 3 2 1
001–345394–March/2025

All rights reserved.
Without limiting the rights under the copyright reserved above, no part of this publication may be reproduced, stored in or introduced into a retrieval system, or transmitted, in any form, or by any means (electronic, mechanical, photocopying, recording, or otherwise), without the prior written permission of the copyright owner. Published in Great Britain by Dorling Kindersley Limited

A catalog record for this book is available from the Library of Congress.
HC ISBN: 978-0-5939-6235-0
PB ISBN: 978-0-5939-6234-3

DK books are available at special discounts when purchased in bulk for sales promotions, premiums, fund-raising, or educational use. For details, contact:
DK Publishing Special Markets, 1745 Broadway, 20th Floor, New York, NY 10019
SpecialSales@dk.com

Printed and bound in China
Super Readers Lexile® levels 310L to 490L
Lexile® is the registered trademark of MetaMetrics, Inc. Copyright © 2024 MetaMetrics, Inc. All rights reserved.

The publisher would like to thank the following for their kind permission to reproduce their images:
a=above; c=center; l=left; r=right; t=top; b/g=background
Depositphotos Inc: Rawpixel 19br; **Dreamstime.com:** Alekss 15ca, 15bc, Yuri Arcurs 27bc, Yana Bardichevska 9tc, 26bl, Boggy 1, Carline1 25t, 30cla, Chernetskaya 18, 30clb, Bonita Cheshier 8cl, 30cl, Michael Flippo 20bl, Aleksei Gorodenkov 6cb, Jenifoto406 8cr, 9cr, 9crb, 13bl, Kewuwu 6bl, Ksuklein 25bl, Lacheev 11b, Richard Lammerts 17br, Monkey Business Images 3, 7, 11cl, 14t, 16b, 17, Picsfive 22 (Balls), Anna Puhan 15clb, Rido 26t, Svetlana Shapiro 14b, Oleksandr Svitlovskyi 20cl (br), Christophe Testi 13ca, Volodymyr Tverdokhlib 8br, Wavebreakmedia Ltd 13b, Yulan 6br, Igor Zakowski 25br; **Getty Images / iStock:** E+ / Alvarez 16t, 19cr, E+ / FatCamera 12, 15bl, E+ / Ferrantraite 10, E+ / Goodboy Picture Company 15c, E+ / Hispanolistic 9t, 30tl, E+ / Kali9 4–5, E+ / Phynart Studio 29, E+ / Skynesher 24c, E+ / SolStock 22, 23, E+ / VeeStudio89 20c, E+ / Xavierarnau 21, Kali9 27cr, Takasuu 24cr, Triloks 6tr; **Shutterstock.com:** Art_Photo 27cl, Chokniti-Studio 28, Graphicfest_X 24br, 30bl

Cover images: *Front:* **Dreamstime.com:** Yuliya Pauliukevich (Background);
Back: **Dreamstime.com:** Sashawallisny (X3)

www.dk.com

Level 1

A DAY IN THE LIFE OF A
TEACHER

Paige Towler

Contents

6	What Does a Teacher Do?
8	Getting Ready
12	Morning Lessons
16	Lunchtime
20	Lots to Learn
26	After School

30 Glossary
31 Index
32 Quiz

What Does a Teacher Do?

A teacher's job is to help people learn. Teachers help us understand the world. They also teach us new skills.

Teachers teach students. Students can be children or adults.

There are many kinds of teachers. Most teachers work in schools.

Getting Ready

Good morning! Teachers get to school before their students do. They plan what they will teach each day.

This teacher uses a notebook called a planner.

This teacher uses a computer to keep track of lessons.

Teachers get the classroom ready. They clean yesterday's lesson off the board. They prepare the supplies their students will need.

Ready!

The students arrive.
This teacher greets his students.
He makes sure everyone is there.

The teacher tells the class what they will be doing that day.

This teacher leads a morning meeting with her students. Sometimes, there are problems in the classroom. The class talks about how to solve them.

Morning Lessons

Many teachers teach a lot of different things each day.

This student is practicing reading. Her teacher helps her learn to read.

Teachers help students learn to write, too. They practice writing. Practice helps students get better.

This teacher shows students how to solve math problems.

This class goes outside. The teacher helps the students explore nature. They learn about science.

Lunchtime

Lunchtime! Students may eat in a cafeteria, in the classroom, or outside.

Teachers get hungry, too!

Some teachers eat lunch together in a room just for teachers.

This teacher eats with her students.

It's time for recess! Students get a break to run and play.

Teachers watch them as they play. They keep students safe.

Sometimes, teachers lead games on the playground.

Lots to Learn

Next, it's time for art class. The art teacher has paint and paintbrushes. She leads a lesson on painting.

¡Hóla! This teacher teaches Spanish. The student is learning to speak a new language.

The class has gone outside for PE.

This teacher has time to plan.

The teacher is still working during this time. This teacher sends emails to students' families and caregivers. She lets them know how the students are doing.

This teacher gives a quiz. Students answer the questions on the quiz. They show what they have learned.

Some teachers give their students homework. It helps them practice things they learn at school.

25

After School

Brring! The bell rings. School is over. Students pack up their things.

Some students stay after school to do extra activities. They play sports. They join clubs. Teachers can help with after-school activities, too.

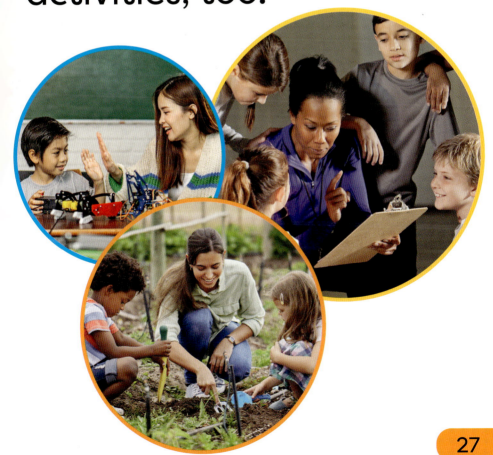

When the day is done, teachers head home. Sometimes, they keep working at home.

This teacher grades quizzes and homework. She checks the answers to see if they are correct.

This teacher is making a lesson for tomorrow. She is excited to teach her students something new.

See you at school!

Glossary

cafeteria
a room in a school where students eat meals

homework
an assignment that students do at home to practice

planner
a special notebook that helps a person stay organized

recess
a break during the school day

quiz
a test of knowledge

Index

after school   26, 27
art class   20
cafeteria   16
computer   8
homework   25, 28
lessons   8, 9, 12, 20, 29
lunchtime   16
math problems   14
meeting   11
outside   15, 16, 22

painting   20
PE   22
plan   8, 23
playground   19
practice   13, 25
quiz   24, 28
reading   12
recess   18
science   15
Spanish   21
writing   13

Quiz

Answer the questions to see what you have learned. Check your answers with an adult.

1. True or False: Students arrive at school before their teachers.
2. What is a cafeteria?
3. True or False: Teachers work only when students are around.
4. How do teachers grade quizzes and homework?
5. Do teachers sometimes keep working after school is over?

1. False 2. A room for eating 3. False 4. They check to see if the answers are correct 5. Yes